Children in The Civil War

A collection of contemporary newspaper stories, anecdotes, etc., illustrated by Alan Archambault

The Boy Father to the Man

When General Grant was a boy, he attended the same school with his cousin John, a Canadian, who had come to the States to be educated. The two youths mingled as relatives; and, whenever the Canadian restrained his inherited prejudices, their intercourse was pleasant. Ulysses felt all the true impulse of patriotism when he was a student at school. It was his conviction, born and nourished in his boy's heart, that his country was the equal of any other and that his countrymen were the equals of the best of mankind. " Speaking of Washington," said his Canadian cousin one day, "it seems to me, Ulysses, you appear to think a great deal of him." " And why shouldn't I?" quickly replied the tanner boy; "he is the father of my country, and was raised up by the Almighty to lead it to independence." " All very fine," retorted John; "but he was a traitor to his king!" " A what?" asked Ulysses, raising his voice.

" Washington was a traitor, a rebel!" continued the Canadian.

" Cousin John," calmly replied Ulysses, "would you like to have your sovereign called hard names?"

" Why, no; I can't say I should."

" Well, then, let me tell you plainly, that I will not allow you or any one to insult the memory of Washington!"

" What are you going to do about it?" queried John with a sneer.

" I shall resent it as I have a right to do. You may take advantage of me; for you are older than I am. My mother has told me not to quarrel with my schoolmates and I mean to mind her, and shall not attack them on my own account. But when Washington is assailed, and especially by an English boy, I shall defend the father of my country. Cousin or no cousin, I am ready to fight for Washington."

So saying, Ulysses laid off his jacket, and soon convinced the Canadian reviler that he was in earnest. Blow quickly followed blow, until young Grant was the victor. The false assertion of the elder boy was corrected and he was compelled to admit that he had done wrong. As he would have defended his own chief ruler, so he was forced to acknowledge that Ulysses had done right in not submitting to hear Washington insulted.

Young Ulysses Grant

Midshipman Farragut

Farragut When a Midshipman

Whatever relates to the career of Admiral Farragut possesses a value to every loyal reader. The following anecdote is therefore given as illustrating the connection between the twig and the tree. When only nine years old, little David determined to be a sailor, and was taken by Commodore Porter on board the *Essex* as a midshipman. He shared the fortunes of that historic craft in her memorable cruises in the Pacific and took part in the battle of Valparaiso.

While that famous contest was at its height, he was ordered by the Commodore to go below and bring up some friction-tubes that were needed for the guns. While descending the ward-room ladder, the captain of the gun directly opposite was struck full in the face by an 18-pounder shot. He fell back against Farragut and they both tumbled down the hatchway. The man was a stout, heavy fellow and it was fortunate for the young midshipman that his full weight did not fall upon him as they reached the deck. As it was, the lad was severely stunned; and recovering as if awakening from a dream, he ran up on the deck. Commodore Porter, seeing him covered with blood, inquired:

" Are you wounded?"

" I believe not," was the reply.

" Then where are the tubes?"

The words brought him to his senses and he immediately went below and got them.

When the brave little brig was surrendered, Farragut sobbed like a child as he saw the American colors hauled down. From this heavy grief he was soon aroused, however, by hearing an English middy exultingly shout to his men, " Prize-oh, boys! Here's a fine grunter, by Jove!" He knew the young reefer alluded to a young porker that had been petted by himself and all the sailors and had helped to beguile away many a weary hour. Therefore, he energetically laid claim to the animal.

" But," said the Englishman, "you're a prisoner, and your pig, too."

" We always respect private property," said Farragut and he seized the squealing bone of contention, asserting that he should retain possession until compelled to yield to superior force. Here was sport for the older officers, who called out:

" Go it, little Yankee; and if you can thrash 'Shorty' (a sobriquet for English middies) you shall have your pig."

" Agreed!" said Farragut, and the lads went at it in pugilistic style. 'Shorty' soon failed to come to time, and the victor walked off with Piggy under his arm. He afterward remarked that he felt, in mastering the young Englishman, that he had wiped out the disgrace of being captured.

Bugler Johnny Cook, Battery B, 4th United States Artillery

Johnny Cook, A Hero of Antietam

Young Johnny Cook was a bugler serving with Battery B, 4th United States Artillery, and he received his nation's highest award: the Medal of Honor for his bravery at the bloody battle of Antietam.

Johnny was born in Hamilton County, Ohio on August 10, 1847 and when the Civil War began he was working as paper boy in Cincinnati. Two months after the rebels fired on Fort Sumter, Johnny enlisted in the Union Army at the tender age of thirteen. On August 28, 1862, Johnny saw his first battle at Brawner Farm, Virginia, where his battery supported the Iron Brigade. Johnny smelled gunpowder again on September 14, 1862 at Turner's Gap, Maryland.

At the Battle of Antietam on September 17, 1862, Battery B again supported the Iron Brigade as they attacked the Confederate positions through Miller's Cornfield. The brigade met fierce resistance and then counterattack. Battery B occupied a knoll west of the Hagerstown Pike and fought the rebels at close range. Confederate shot and shell struck down many of the Union cannoneers as well as the battery's commander. In the midst of the carnage, Johnny rushed to a cannon and took the place of a fallen comrade. The rebels made three attacks against Johnny's gun but were blasted back each time. For his bravery that day Johnny was awarded the Medal of Honor.

When his enlistment expired in 1864, Johnny joined the Union Navy and served on a gunboat until 1865. Following the Civil War, Johnny became a police court reporter in Cincinnati and later found employment at the Government Printing Office in Washington, D.C. Johnny passed into history in 1915 and was laid to rest in Arlington National Cemetery.

Billy Shelton, the Martyr Patriot Boy

The sway of the rebels in East Tennessee was characterized by a trail of blood which flowed from the veins of men, women and children alike. The case of poor little Billy Shelton, the patriot martyr boy, will never cease to be remembered and wept over by every true Union heart. He was but a mere child, twelve years old, but with five others was ordered to kneel and receive the assassin's fire. The soldiers received the order to fire. Poor little Billy was shot in both arms. " You have killed my old father and my three brothers; you have shot me in both arms - I forgive you all this - I can get well. Let me go home to my mother and sisters." His appeal was disregarded.

Safeguard for Body and Soul

Charlie Merrill, a young Massachusetts soldier, had an ounce ball pass through his head during the battle of Fredericksburg. It entered near his right eye and was extracted from behind his left ear. Another ball would have entered a vital part of his body had it not been arrested by a Testament, in which it lodged. When this safeguard was shown to the President, he sent to the hospital a handsome pocket Bible in which, as an evidence of his warm regard, he caused to be inscribed: " Charles W. Merrill, Co. A., 19th Massachusetts, from A. Lincoln."

The Bible Saves Pvt. Merrill

Clever Dogs, But Both Sucked Eggs

During General Birney's raid through Florida, a bright little girl was found alone in one of the houses, her parents having 'skedaddled.' She was rather non-committal, for she did not know whether the troops were Union or rebel. Two fine dogs made their appearance while a conversation was being held with the child, and she informed one of her questioners that their names were Gillmore and Beauregard. " Which is the best dog?" asked a bystander. " I don't know," said she, " they're both mighty smart dogs; but they'll either of 'em suck eggs if you don't watch 'em." The troops left without ascertaining whether the family, of which the girl was a hopeful scion, was Union or rebel.

A Clever Girl

The Lieutenant's Perfumed Breath

Little Freddy H., a four-year-old son of Chaplain H., of a New York regiment of volunteers, perpetrated a good thing while his father's regiment was at camp at Suffolk. A smart-looking Lieutenant, with dashing air and *perfumed breath,* went inside a tent where Freddy was. The little soldier scanned him very closely, and when a convenient opportunity offered itself he said to the Lieutenant, " You are a *doctor;* I *know* you are a *doctor.*" " No, my little man," replied the officer, " you are mistaken *this* time; I am not a doctor." " Yes, you are a *doctor,* too!" replied Freddy; " I know you are a doctor; *for I can smell the medicine!*" This was too good a thing to be kept, and half an hour did not elapse before it had spread throughout the regiment.

A Smart Young Nose

The Brave Drummer Boy

Orion P. Howe of Waukegan, Illinois, drummer-boy to the Fifty-fifth Volunteers of that state, was appointed to fill a vacancy in the Naval School at Newport. The following extract, from a letter written by Major-General Sherman to Secretary Stanton detailing an incident which transpired during the assault upon the rebel works at Vicksburg on May 19th, doubtless secured the boy's promotion:

" When the assault at Vicksburg was at its height on the 19th of May, and I was in front near the road which formed my line of attack, this young lad came up to me wounded and bleeding, with a good, healthy boy's cry: ' Gen. Sherman, send some cartridges to Col. Malmborg, the men are nearly all out.' ' What is the matter, my boy?' ' They shot me in the leg, sir, but I can go to the hospital. Send the cartridges right away.' Even where we stood, the shot fell thick, and I told him to go to the rear at once. I would attend to the cartridges, and off he limped. Just before he disappeared over the hill, he turned around and shouted as loud as he could: ' Calibre 54.' I have not seen the lad since, and his Colonel, Malmborg, on inquiry, gives me his address as above and says he is a bright, intelligent boy with a fair preliminary education.

" What arrested my attention then was, and what renews my memory of the fact now is, that one so young, carrying a musket-ball wound through his leg, should have found his way to me on that fatal spot and delivered his message, not forgetting the very important part of the calibre of his musket, 54, which you know is an unusual one.

" I'll warrant that the boy has in him the elements of a man, and I commend him to the Government as one worthy the fostering care of some one of its national institutions."

Drummer Boy Howe and General Sherman

A Baby on the Battlefield

At the battle of the Hatchie, when the conflict was waging fiercest, upon advancing midway between the contending forces, we found - what do you think? Not a masked battery, not an insidious trap, not any terrible engine of death, but a sweet little blue-eyed *baby*! Sweet little thing, as I saw it there, hugging the cold earth, its only bed, a little tear on its cheek -

" That nature bade it weep, turned
An ice-drop sparkling in the morning beam."

Unalarmed amid the awful confusion of that fearsome battle, with the missiles of death flying thick about it and crowding close upon its young existence, yet unhurt, it seemed a wonderful verification of the Divine declaration: " Out of the mouths of babes and sucklings I will ordain wisdom." That little " child of war," as it lay in its miraculous safety, seemed to say to me these words of profound instruction: " My helplessness and innocence appealed to God and He preserved me in the midst of this wrecking carnage. If you will make your plaint to Heaven, God will preserve your poor bleeding country."

Little child of destiny, born amid the flash of musketry, the thunder of cannon, and the clash of arms, I will watch your course through life and witness whether an existence so auspiciously begun will pass by the masses unnoticed and end without leaving a name " damned to everlasting fame!" Who would suppose that in the wild, fierce battle of the Hatchie, when the field was strewn with the dead and the shrieks of the wounded rent the Heavens with agony, a great army would pause in the thickest of the conflict to save a harmless, helpless child? Yet the brave Fourteenth, that never yet has quailed in battle, did pause, and an officer of the regiment ordered " our little baby" carried to headquarters and tenderly cared for.

I remember having read somewhere in Grecian history a story something like the one I have related. A little child was found on the battlefield and trampled in the dust by an infuriated soldiery. After the battle, the victorious general in an address to his army said, " But for the blood of a *little child* that mars it, our victory would be complete." Thank God the blood of no little child mars our victory.

The next day after the battle, " our baby" was brought before the Fourteenth and unanimously adopted " Child of the Regiment." Three or four days later, strange as it would seem, a poor, heart-stricken, poverty-pinched mother came searching the battlefield in quest for her child. My dear reader, imagine if you can the wild exclamations of thanks that burst from that poor woman's heart when informed that her child had been rescued and with a mother's tenderness cared for. I saw the mother receive her child, heard her brief prayer for the soldiers who saved it, and with the blessing of a thousand men following her and hers, she took away

" Our little baby - little blue-eyed, laughing baby."

“Lookee Thar!”

Little Eddie the Drummer Boy

A few days before our regiment received orders to join General Lyons on his march to Wilson's Creek, the drummer of our company was taken sick and conveyed to the hospital, and on the evening preceding the day that we were to march, a black man was arrested within the lines of our camp and brought before our captain, who asked him, "What business do you have among the lines?" He replied, " I know a drummer that you would like to enlist in your company, and I have come to tell you of it." He was immediately requested to inform the drummer that if he would enlist for our short term of service, he would be allowed extra pay and to do this, he must be on the ground early in the morning. The black man was then passed beyond the guard.

On the following morning there appeared before the captain's quarters a good-looking, middle-aged woman, dressed in deep mourning, leading by the hand a sharp, sprightly-looking boy, twelve years old. Her story was soon told. She was from east Tennessee, where her husband had been killed by the rebels, and all their property destroyed. She had come to St. Louis in search of her sister, but not finding her and being destitute, she thought if she could procure a situation for her boy as a drummer for the short time we had to remain in the service, she could find employment for herself, and perhaps find her sister by the time we were discharged.

During the rehearsal of her story the little fellow kept his eyes intently fixed upon the countenance of the captain, who was about to express a determination not to take so small a boy, when he spoke out: "Don't be afraid, Captain, I can drum." This was spoken with so much confidence that the captain immediately observed with a smile, " Well, well, sergeant, bring the drum, and order our piper to come forward." In a few moments the drum was produced, and a tall, round-shouldered, good-natured fellow, from the Dubuque mines, who stood something over six feet in height, soon made his appearance.

Upon being introduced to his new comrade, he stooped down with his hands resting on his knees, and after peering into the little fellow's face a moment, he observed, " My little man, can you drum?" " Yes, sir," he replied. " I drummed for Captain Hill in Tennessee." Our piper immediately commenced straightening himself upward until all the angles in his body had disappeared. He placed his pipe at his mouth and played " The Flowers of Edinburgh," one of the most difficult things to follow with the drum that could have been selected, and nobly did the little fellow follow him, showing himself to be a master of the drum. When the music ceased, our captain turned to the mother and said, " Madam, I will take your boy. What is his name?" " Edward Lee," she replied; then placing her hand upon the captain's arm, she continued: " Captain, you will bring him back with you, won't you?"

" Yes, yes," he replied, " we will be certain to bring him back with us. We shall be discharged in six weeks."

Eddie from Tennessee of the Iowa First

An hour later, our company led the Iowa First out of camp, our drum and pipe playing. Eddie, as we called him, soon became a great favorite with all the men in the company. When any of the boys returned from a horticultural excursion, Eddie's share of the peaches and melons was the first apportioned out. During our heavy and fatiguing march from Rolla to Springfield, it was often amusing to see our long-legged piper wading through the mud with our drummer boy mounted upon his back, and always in that position when fording streams.

During the fight at Wilson's Creek I was stationed with a part of our company on the right of Totten's battery while the balance of our company, with a part of the Illinois regiment, was ordered down into a deep ravine on our left, in which it was known a portion of the enemy lay concealed, with whom they were soon engaged. The contest in the ravine continuing some time, Totten suddenly wheeled his battery upon the enemy in that quarter when they soon retreated to the high ground behind their lines. In less than twenty minutes after, Totten had driven the enemy from the ravine, the word passed from man to man throughout the army, " Lyon is killed!" and soon after, hostilities having ceased upon both sides, the order came for our main force to fall back upon Springfield, while part of the Iowa First and two companies of the Missouri regiment were to camp upon the ground and cover the retreat next morning. That night I was detained for guard duty, my turn of guard closing with the morning call. When I went out with the officer as a relief, I found that my post was upon a high eminence that overlooked the deep ravine in which our men had engaged the enemy, until Totten's battery came to their assistance. It was a dreary, lonesome beat. The moon had gone down in the early part of the night while the stars twinkled dimly through a hazy atmosphere, lighting up imperfectly the surrounding objects. Occa sionally I would place my ear near the ground and listen for the sound of footsteps, but all was silent save for the far-off howling of the wolf, that seemed to scent upon the evening air the banquet that we had been preparing for him. The hours passed slowly away, when at length the morning light began to streak along the eastern sky, making surroundings plainly visible. Presently I heard a drum beat out the morning call. At first I thought it came from the camp of the enemy across the creek; but as I listened, I found that it came up from the deep ravine; for a few minutes it was silent, and then as it became more light I heard it again. I listened - the sound of the drum was familiar to me - and I knew that it was

Our drummer boy from Tennessee
Beating for help the *réveille*.

I was about to desert my post to go to his assistance when I discovered the officer of the guard approaching with two men. We all listened to the sound and were satisfied that it was Eddie's drum. I asked permission to go to his assistance. The officer hesitated, saying that the orders were to march in twenty minutes. I promised to be back in that time, and he consented. I immediately started down the hill through the thick undergrowth and upon reaching the valley I followed the sound of the drum, and soon found him seated upon the ground, his back leaning against the trunk of a fallen tree, while his drum hung upon a bush in front of him, reaching nearly to the ground. As soon as he discovered me, he dropped his drumsticks and exclaimed, " O Corporal! I am so glad to see you! Give me a drink," reaching out his hand for my canteen, which was empty. I immediately turned to bring him some water from the brook that I could hear rippling through the bushes nearby, when, thinking that I was about to leave him, he commenced crying, saying, " Don't leave me, Corporal! I can't walk." I was soon back with the water, when I discovered that both of his feet had been shot away by a cannon-ball. After satisfying his thirst, he looked up into my face and said: " You don't think I will die, Corporal, do you? This man said I would not - he said the surgeon could cure my feet." I now discovered a man lying in the grass near him. By his dress I recognized him as belonging to the enemy. It appeared that he had been shot through the bowels, and fallen near where Eddie lay. Knowing that he could not live, and seeing the condition of the boy, he had crawled to him, taken off his buckskin suspenders, and corded the little fellow's legs below the knee, and then died. While he was telling me these particulars, I heard the tramp of cavalry coming down the ravine, and in a moment a scout of the enemy was upon us, and I was taken prisoner. I requested the officer to take Eddie up in front of him, and he did so, carrying him with great tenderness and care. When we reached the camp of the enemy the little fellow was dead.

Two Boys Capture a Reb

Intrepid Conduct of Two Drummer Boys

Two drummer boys of the Tenth Connecticut Volunteers, while off duty, and while Gillmore was pounding Fort Wagner, determined to discover the effect made upon the fort, and for this purpose borrowed an opera glass and went out to obtain a favorable site to witness the operations. They had proceeded about three quarters of a mile, when they came suddenly upon a burly rebel who, upon sight of the boys, snapped his gun at them, which however did not explode, the piece not being capped. One of the boys at that moment, thrusting the glass into the case which hung at his side, the rebel thought he was drawing a revolver, and immediately threw down his gun, crying out, " I surrender!" The boys immediately sprang forward, seized his gun, and at a "charge bayonet" drove the big fellow into camp. When he discovered that the only weapon in the boys' possession was an opera glass, he was much incensed, declaring he could not be held as a prisoner of war. The fact was witnessed by the Colonel of the regiment, who highly commended the intrepid conduct of the boys.

Three Soldiers Captured by a Boy with a Coffee Pot

An amusing instance of the value of a ready wit and presence of mind occurred during the advance of the Second Corps of Federal troops near Hatcher's Run. A young lad in the Fourteenth Connecticut regiment, going with a coffee-pot to get water from the stream, suddenly found himself surrounded by three of the enemy. With all the fierceness of voice the little fellow could muster, he commanded them to throw down their arms and surrender. Supposing that the brave youth had companions near to enforce his command, they complied, when he seized one of their muskets and marched them into camp in great triumph. This story was related in his camp as the capture of three Johnnies with a coffee-pot.

Beware of a Yankee Boy with a Coffee Pot

Uniforms: all gray. Flag: white field, gold fringe,
Old Glory (still on the flag), blue scroll with gold letters.

Cadets of the Virginia Military Institute

One of the most inspiring and dramatic incidents of the Civil War occurred in the Shenandoah Valley of Virginia in the Spring of 1864. As General Franz Sigel led his Union army through the valley, Confederate General John C. Breckinridge called on the teen-age students of the Virginia Military Institute to fill the ranks of his struggling forces. On Sunday, May 15, 1864, 264 young cadets gallantly charged a Union battery at the battle of New Market. They captured a Union cannon and several prisoners in hand-to-hand combat. They proudly carried their cherished flag into the battle and, later, when Union forces burned the school, they cut the flag into pieces and gave them to all the cadets to prevent it from falling into Yankee hands. Five young cadets were killed at the battle of New Market and five more died later of their wounds. Each year on May 15, the present-day cadets hold a special ceremony to honor those cadets who fell at New Market.

John Lincoln Clem

One of the smallest yet bravest soldiers in the Union Army was Johnny Clem. In May 1861, at the age of nine, he ran away from home and tried to join the Union Army. Although he was turned away by several units, he tagged along after the 22nd Michigan and performed camp duties for the men. Even though he was not officially mustered in, the officers and men chipped in to pay him $13 a month. Johnny first won fame at the battle of Shiloh where his drum was smashed by an artillery shell. Later, at the battle of Chickamauga, Johnny shot an attacking Confederate officer. After this he began to be known as the "Drummer Boy of Chickamauga." Johnny eventually became a courier and was wounded twice. Following the war, he was appointed a second lieutenant in the Regular Army and retired from the service in 1916 as a major general.

Johnny Clem at the Battle of Chickamauga

Black Children in Service to the Union

From the very beginning of the Civil War, the black population of the South sensed that the war would bring them freedom. At every opportunity, black men, women and children would do what they could to help the Union forces achieve victory. Black children often served as guides and spies for the Union and would help wounded Union soldiers. Many Union prisoners, who escaped from the Rebels, were helped by black children and adults. The slaves helped the soldiers avoid Confederate patrols and led them back to Union lines. Although most of their exploits went unrecorded, many Union veterans testified to the brave and dedicated service of black patriots.

Black Children Help a Union Soldier

Albert, Drummer Boy of the Massachussetts 23rd

Albert Munson of Marblehead was a little hero, fifteen years of age, who could merrily play Yankee Doodle and the Star-Spangled Banner and, struck by his bold and inspiring manner, Colonel Kurtz appointed him as a drummer in one of the companies of the Massachusetts Twenty-third. His father was attached to the same regiment.

They sailed in the Burnside expedition and at the battle of Roanoke Island, after a weary march through slime and water, they came in sight of the enemy's battery. " Who will go and take it?" asked the General commanding. " The Massachusetts Twenty-third," was the quick reply. " Forward, then, double-quick!" and in the teeth of a galling fire they rushed to their death as if it had been to their bridal. The father fell wounded by his side, but the son heeded him not; his whole soul had lost itself in the work before him. " Look at that child!" said one officer to another; " No wonder we conquer when boys fight so."

" Didn't I say they should run to the old tunes?" and seizing a disabled revolver for a drum-stick, he struck up, in a wondrously defiant way, our impudent old strain of Yankee Doodle. A flying rebel heard it, and looking back, took sure aim at Albert. A man near the boy saw the deadly aim and tried to pull Albert down, but he stood his ground and the ball did not fail to do its fatal work. His knightly Colonel's arms held the brave boy and all bent eagerly to hear his last words: " Which beat? Quick, tell me!" Tears ran down the blackened faces, and one, in a voice husky with sobs, said, " We, Albert, the field is ours." " Why don't you go after 'em? Don't mind me, I'll catch up - I'm a little cold, but running will warm me."

Red, White, and Blue - God's Flag

When the Federal troops first made their appearance near Bardstown, Kentucky, a little boy, who had just discovered a beautiful rainbow arching the heavens, ran to his mother and exclaimed, " Mother, God is a Union man." His mother questioned him about his reason for thinking so, and the little fellow replied that he had seen His flag, and it was " Red, White, and Blue." Surely, "out of the mouths of babes and sucklings hast thou ordained strength because of thine enemies."

Great Act for a Little Girl

Mr. Herbert, a kind-hearted farmer in Illinois, had a little daughter, who, upon hearing her father ask others to give for in aid of the sick and wounded soldiers, thought of what she could do. Of all her playthings she had nothing which could be sold for any amount and so bring money. But she had a very sweet pet lamb, almost as dear to her as a brother or sister. That surely would bring something. It was of the very finest stock. She had taught it many cunning tricks and winsome ways. The two, child and lamb, had eaten from the same dish, and many hours they had played together on the sunny hillside. The lamb, like "Little Mary's", also knew its name as well as that of its mistress. She proposed, with tears in her eyes, and almost heart-broken to think of it, to give her dear pet to the sick and wounded soldiers. She gave it, and she and the lamb together went in the procession on one of the wagons. The president of the Soldiers' Home gave twenty-five dollars for the lamb, and in his speech at the dinner, said he should prize it very much, and through the incident teach his own daughter a lesson. After they had placed the lamb in a large box to be sent to its purchaser's country residence, its former little mistress took leave of it, fondling and kissing her dear pet. With her eyes full of tears she said she was very sorry to part with it, because it loved her and she loved it so very much. - but, the soldiers needed the money more than she needed the lamb because they sometimes lost their limbs and sometimes were killed. Taking all the circumstances into consideration, it was a great act for a little girl.

She Helped Save the Union

My Bold Soldier Boy

" What do the women say about us boys at home?" asked a poor battle-wrecked soldier in the hospital, himself but a lad, of one who sat at his side. That brow of his ached for the touch of a loving hand. He had walked through rough, stony places - temptation, sin, folly had beset him on the right hand and on the left; but he still felt a mother's influence on his soul, leading him into the June paths of old. At the very moment he asked the question, " What do the women say of us at home?" he was turning over a silken needle-book that some laughing girl had one day sent to the Sanitary Commission, working on its cover the words, playfully, perhaps, " My bold soldier boy." The friend, sitting by, simply pointed to the happy inscription. The reply struck home to his heart and he burst into tears. They were not bitter tears, but tears of joy. His question was answered; the evidence of woman's interest was before his eyes, and he was content. His eyelids closed down, his breathing grew calm, and soon sleep touched him, and he was dreaming.

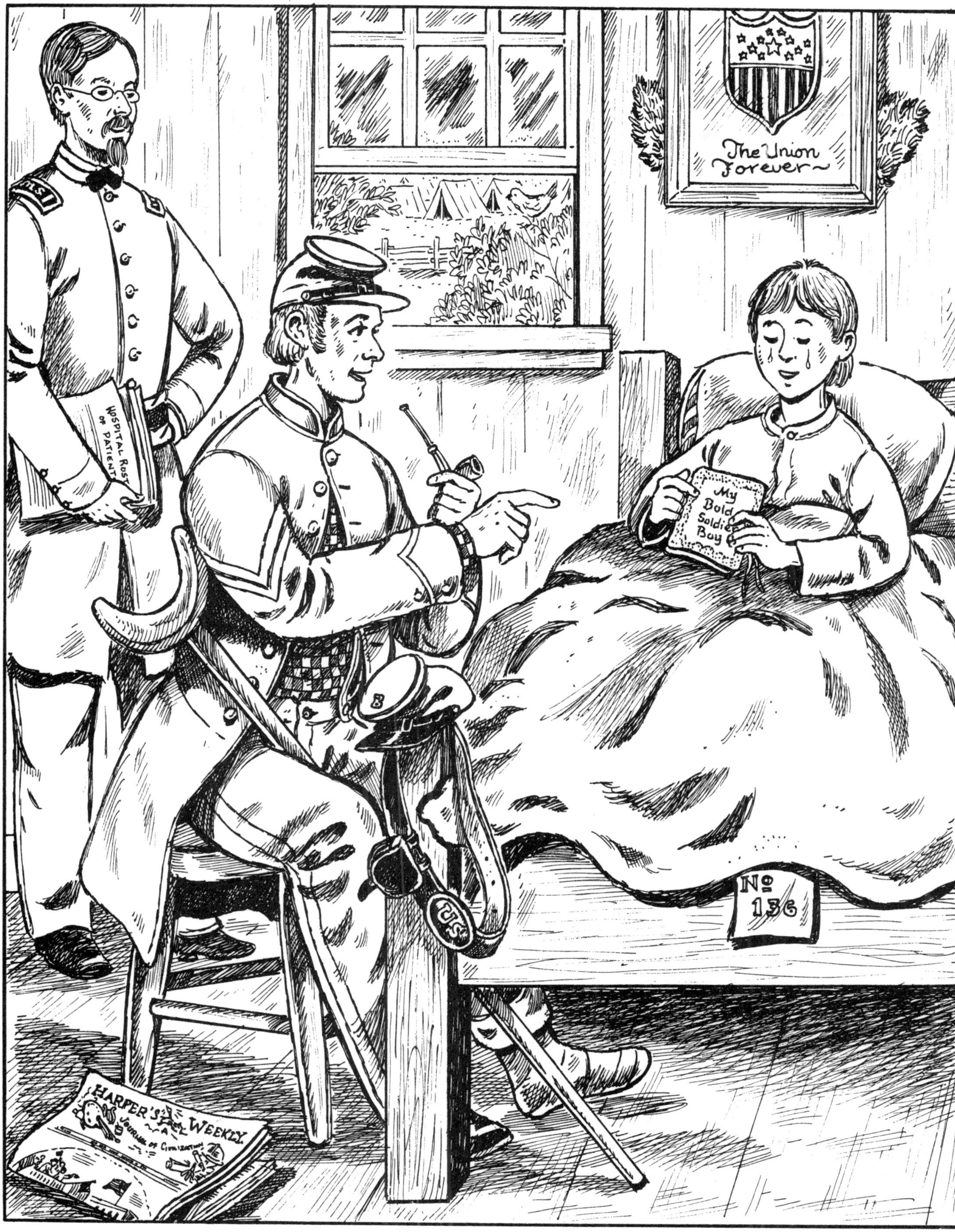

A Loving Message for a Brave Boy

A Union Boy and Rebel Lads

Boy Soldiers at the Old Ones' Trade

Knoxville, Tennessee, is a town well known. Across a little creek is a place called Shieldstown. The spirit of war exhibited itself warmly among the boys six, eight, and ten years old, and the fight raged fiercely between the Shieldstowners and Knoxvillers. They used slings and minié balls which they handled with great dexterity. They had campfires built along in a line. Every morning each party appeared on its own side of the stream, drawn up in array. Ammunition was distributed out of a bag, fifteen rounds to the man, and they commenced. Old soldiers of the Ninth Corps, who had been through many a storm of shot and shell, kept at a respectable distance as they hurled their miniés with vigor. One day the Shieldstowners made a charge at the single plank that crossed the stream. The Knoxvillers ran for dear life, all except one little fellow about eight years old. He stood at the end of the plank, swearing oaths like Parrott shells, calling them cowards, and by a vigorous discharge of miniés repulsed the assault. The casualties amounted to bruises and cuts in all parts of the body, rather serious to look at, or to think what they might have been; but every little fellow was proud of his wound. So it went on for several days when one bright morning, as they were drawn up in full fighting array and awaiting the military signal to commence, suddenly some women appeared in rear of each fighting party. A half dozen would-be soldiers were caught up, severely spanked, and led off. The rest were disconcerted and dispersed.

An Admonishing Young Rebel Captain

He was Too Big Not to be a Soldier

When the present war commenced (says a contributor to Harper's Drawer), I was practicing law in the State of Georgia. I was a strong Union man, and concluded to leave the land of secession and return to my native city. I started for Mobile to run the blockade; when I reached Montgomery, Alabama, I found I would have to remain until the next day. That evening, after tea, there was a large crowd in the rotunda of the hotel, and the war was, of course, the general theme of conversation. " War! War to the death!" was nearly the only expression that could be heard. Everybody was volunteering and the whole city seemed to be in uniform. In the midst of the excitement a little boy, about five years old, came out of one of the parlors, dressed in the full uniform of a Confederate Captain. He looked so pretty and smart that I patted him on the head, saying, " You're a very little man to be a soldier." He turned, measured me with his eye, and replied, " You're a very *big* man *not* to be a soldier!" The crowd appreciated it, and I paid for the liquor.

Eleven-Year-Old Warrior Picking Off the Enemy

A boy about eleven years old cut what might be called a tall figure in the Fort Donelson fight. His father, a volunteer, had been taken prisoner by the Confederates some time previously. The boy smuggled himself on board one of the transports at Cincinnati, laden with troops for the scene of the conflict. On the field, the morning of the great fight, he joined the Seventy-eighth Ohio, and being questioned by one of the officers, he told him of his father having been taken prisoner, and having no mother, he had no one to care for him, and he wanted to fight his father's captors. The officer tried to get him to turn back, but he was not to be denied. So he succeeded in obtaining a musket and went into the thickest of the battle. He finally by degrees crept up within a short distance of the Confederate intrenchments and posted himself behind a tree, from which he kept firing as often as he could see a head to fire at. He was soon discovered by the enemy's sharpshooters who endeavored to drive him away from his position, as he kept picking them off very frequently. One of the seccessionists, who was outside of the work, got sight of the boy with his rifle, but before he got his piece off, the little warrior fired, and down went Mr. Rebel. As the latter had a fine Minié rifle, the boy ran out and picked it up, taking time to get pouch and balls, together with his knapsack, while the bullets were flying on all sides of him, and then he retreated to his wooden breastwork where he renewed his fire, with a little better success. After being in the fight all day he returned to the Seventy-eighth at night with his prizes. This story might appear incredible for one so young to be the hero, but it is vouched for by a number of officers and men who saw the boy on the field and in the position mentioned, and many saw him shoot the man referred to, besides several others.

A Boy of the 78th Ohio

Young Harry Captured 25 Men at Gettysburg

Well Done for a Youth

The gallant conduct of Henry Shaler of Indianapolis, Indiana, at the battle of Gettysburg, was worthy of all praise and remembrance. He seems to have more than equaled the self-told mythical performance of the Irishman who "surrounded" a half-dozen of the enemy and bagged them plump. Henry's parents resided in Indianapolis and were Germans. Harry was a brick; he did more, that is, he took more prisoners in the battle of Gettysburg than any other man in the army. He took twenty-five men in all - one lieutenant and eighteen men at one time. He took them by strategy that was strategy - he surrounded them, and they had to give up. On the morning of the fourth he went out with his poncho over his shoulders, so that the rebs couldn't see his coat, and thus they thought he was one of their own men. He went up and told them to lay down their arms and come and help carry some wounded off the field; they did so. When he got them away from their arms he rode up to the Lieutenant and told him to give up his sword; the lieutenant refused at first, but Harry drew his pepper-box and, like Crockett's coon, the lieutenant came down without a shot. Harry then took them all into camp. He took a captain and five men at another time, making twenty-five in all. Pretty well for little Harry - one of Meade's noblest fighters.

Them and Theirs - Not Us

One of the most interesting cases among the rebel prisoners at Camp Denison, Ohio, was a wounded youth whose heart was evidently busy doing poetic justice to the Yankees he had been taught to hate, though he still was anxious about Southern rights. Parson Clayton talked to him for some time concerning religious matters and the young man at last broke in by saying, " We've talked about religion long enough, now let's talk politics." There was a peculiar Southernism about his look and tone that excited a smile all around. " Well," replied Mr. Clayton, " I'm not much on politics; I'd rather not talk about them - tell me how you felt when you were wounded." He did so.

" Thought it would be a sharp pain, Sir, but it wasn't. I was wounded in the legs, and it was just like my being knocked off my pins by a strong blow from a log of wood. Fell flat on my belly, and my knees drew themselves up under my chin. Made sure I was dead, but thought it didn't make much difference, for I saw our men retreating and knew that the Yankees would get me and kill me sure; always was told, Sir, the Yankees had horns. Well, there I lay; and up came a Colonel leading his men - he was in front, Sir. He jumped down from his horse and ran to me drawing something from his belt, so I gave up; but it wasn't a pistol, Sir," (and here the boy's eyes moistened) "it was a canteen! He put it to my lips; I drank. He jumped on his horse again and said, ' Charge, boys, they're fleeing!' Then some soldiers on foot came towards me and I thought, 'They're not all like that officer,' and I gave up again. But Sir, they said, ' Comrade, get up.' They lifted me up and said, ' Put your arms around our necks and we'll lead you away from these bullets.' And these were the 'damned Yankees!' I tell you, Sir, no man ever hugged his sweetheart harder or more friendly than I hugged those Yankees' necks."

After a few more remarks the youth showed a determination to "talk politics" and asked Mr. Clayton, " What are you fighting us for?" Mr. Clayton calmly, and in good humor, gave him his ideas of the issue, and in ending asked him what they were fighting for. " To hold property, Sir," replied the youth , "Our slave property." " How many slaves did you have?" " None." " And you?" (to the next). " None." He then went around to all the thirty-four rebels and but one was found who owned a slave. "Now," said Mr. Clayton, "where are the men who have these slaves which they are so afraid of losing?" Here a man named McLellan, who soon afterwards died, raised himself up on his cot, and stretching out his thin hand said in a sepulchral voice, " They are at home enjoying themselves and have sent *us* to die for them and theirs." And to this the echoes around the room were, " That's so!" " That's God's truth!"

The Yankees Didn't Have Horns After All

Bob, the Spunky Drummer Boy

The Battle of Fredericksburg was attended by many memorable instances of individual heroism. It is known that for several days a curtain of thick fog rose up from the waters of the Rappahannock, completely hiding from view the artillery that crowned the opposite hills and the infantry that crowded the sheltering ravines. But the preparation for the great fight, so hopefully commenced, was continued amid the thunder of cannon and the eruptions of exploding batteries.

The hazardous work of laying the pontoon bridges was frequently interrupted by the murderous fire of the Confederate sharpshooters, concealed in the stores and dwelling-houses on the bank of the river. To dislodge these men and drive them out of their hiding places seemed an impossible task. At a given signal, the Union batteries opened with a terrific fire upon the city, crashing through the walls of houses and public buildings. But in this storm of shot and shell which ploughed the streets and set the buildings on fire, the sharpshooters survived, like salamanders in the flames, and continued to pour a deadly fire upon the Federal engineers and bridge-builders.

In this dilemma it became evident that the bridges could not be laid except by a bold dash. Volunteers were called for to cross in small boats; forthwith, hundreds stepped forth and offered their services. One hundred men were chosen and at once started for the boats. Robert Henry Hendershot was then a member of the Eighth Michigan - acting as a drummer boy. Seeing a part of the Seventh Michigan preparing to cross the river, he ran ahead and leaped into the boat. One of the officers ordered him out, saying he would be shot. The boy replied that he didn't care, that he was willing to die for his country. When the boy found that the captain would not permit him to remain in the boat, he begged the privilege of pushing the boat off, and the request was granted. Whereupon, instead of remaining on shore, he clung to the stern of the boat and, submerged to the waist in water, he crossed the Rappahannock. Soon as he landed, a fragment of a shell struck his old drum and knocked it to pieces. Picking up a musket, he went in search of relics and obtained a secesh flag, a clock, a knife, and a bone ring. On opening a back door in one of the enemy's houses, he found a Confederate soldier who was wounded in the hand, and ordered him to surrender. He did so and was taken by the boy-soldier to the Seventh Michigan. When the drummer boy recrossed the river from Fredericksburg, General Burnside said to him, in the presence of the army:

" Boy, I glory in your spunk; if you keep on this way a few more years, you will be in my place."

Young Bob and General Burnside at the Battle of Fredericksburg

Young Wainwright

The following incident is given in an account by a Confederate prisoner who participated in the capture of the U.S. ship Harriet Lane:

Almost the first men to be struck down were the gallant Captain Wainwright and Lieutenant Lee, who both fought with a desperation and valor no mortal could surpass. Though bleeding and prostrate upon the deck, they were seen continuing to deal death among their enemies. One young son of Captain Wainwright - only ten years old! - stood at the cabin door, a revolver in each hand, and never ceased firing until he had expended every shot. One of his poor little hands became disabled by a ball, shattering four fingers, and then his infantile soul gave way. He burst into tears and cried, ' Do you want to kill me?" Blessed young hero! May his country never forget him! And where is the Hemans to wed his name to immortal verse, like another Cassabianca, or the artist to portray the scene on historic canvas?

Childhood's Prayer in the Last Hour

It was the evening after a great battle. All day long the din of strife had echoed far, and thickly strewn lay the shattered forms of those so lately erect and exultant in the flush and strength of manhood. Among the many who bowed to the conqueror Death that night was a youth in the first freshness of mature life. The strong limbs lay listless and the dark hair was matted with gore on the pale, broad forehead. His eyes were closed. As one who ministered to the sufferer bent over him, he at first thought the young man was dead, but the white lips moved and slowly in weak tones he repeated, " Now I lay me down to sleep," etc., going through those five sweet and precious lines.

As he finished he opened his eyes and, meeting the pitying gaze of a brother soldier, he exclaimed, " My mother taught me that when I was a little boy and I have said it every night since I can remember. Before the morning dawns, I believe that God will take my soul for Jesus' sake, but before I die I want to send a message to my mother."

He was carried to a temporary hospital and a letter was written to his mother which he dictated, full of Christian faith and filial love. He was calm and peaceful. Just as the sun rose, his spirit went home. His last articulate words were, " I pray the Lord my soul to take, and this I ask for Jesus' sake." The prayer of childhood was thus the prayer of manhood. He learned it at his mother's knee in his distant Northern home and he whispered it in dying, when his young life ebbed away on a Southern battlefield.

The Little Girl's Kindness to the Soldiers

" After the battle of Sharpsburg, we passed over a line of railroad in Central Georgia. The disabled soldiers from General Lee's armies were returning to their homes.

" We shall never forget how very like an angel was a little girl - how blushingly and modestly she went to a great, rude, bearded soldier, who had carved a crutch from a rough plank to replace a lost leg; how this little girl asked him if he was hungry - and how he ate like a famished wolf! She asked if his wound was painful, and in a voice of soft, mellow accents, ' Can I do nothing more for you? I am sorry that you are so badly hurt; have you a little daughter, and won't she cry when she sees you?' The rude soldier's heart was touched, and tears of love and gratitude filled his eyes. He only answered, ' I have three little children; God grant they may be such angels as you.' " — *Southern paper*